W9-BMO-737

Philip Howard

Father&
an intimate study
Son

Published by

Family First

Lincoln, Nebraska

Family First

The Nebraska Center for Family Policy
PO Box 82114
Lincoln, NE 68501-2114

Manufactured in the United States of America

Library of Congress Cataloging-in-Publication Data
Philip E. Howard.
        Father & Son: An Intimate Study / Philip E. Howard.

        ISBN 0-9671260-0-2

99-62054
CIP

FATHER & SON

Contents

Foreword

On many a Sunday afternoon when there were still only three of us children, we visited Grandpa and Grandma Howard in their apartment on West School Lane in Philadelphia. As we came up the stairs (where there was always a farrago of cooking smells) we were greeted with Grandma's delighted "Well for *pity's sake!*" or Grandpa's "Just look who's *here!*" Lots of hugs? No, there was none of that in our day. We wouldn't have known what to do with them.

We understood that Mother and Daddy wanted to talk with the old folks and we young folks were to amuse ourselves quietly. There were interesting things to look at. In Grandpa's tiny study there was a crown of thorns, a replica of the one with which the sneering soldiers crowned the Lord Jesus. There was a painting of the face of Jesus, fascinating because if you looked at it one way, His eyes seemed to be looking tenderly at us, but in another way, they appeared closed, as though He were praying. (I have this is my own study today.) Over the desk there was a motto, "**NOT SOMEHOW BUT TRIUMPHANTLY,**" each letter written on a little wooden block, all suspended from a string. This I memorized as a fortifying principle in my life, but as I look back I'm afraid there have been more than a few occasions of "not triumphantly but somehow"!

And there were books. Oh, there were books all over the place—in the study, in the living room and bedrooms and lining the hallway so that you almost had to turn sideways to walk. I often settled myself on the hall floor and read Aunt Anne's girls' books.

In the hall there was a stand that held umbrellas and canes. One Sunday my brothers Phil and Dave took it into their heads to take one of the canes, a finely carved one, outdoors. Of course I trotted along. They jammed it into the ground and in trying to yank it out managed to break it right in half. A major disaster. How to confess this crime? Daddy was very upset indeed. Did he spank anybody? I can't remember, but I'm sure Grandpa and Grandma made light of the whole thing. They were truly gentle people and took the spoiling of their goods joyfully. I have no recollection whatsoever of anything but lovingkindness toward us from both.

We never heard much about our great-grandfather Eugene Howard, but we heard many stories about great-grandfather Henry Clay Trumbull, a leader in the Sunday School movement, chaplain in the Civil War and author of many books including HINTS ON CHILD TRAINING. He had eight children, one of whom was my ("Well, for *pity's sake!"*) grandmother, Annie Slosson Trumbull. Her father's influence on his son-in-law was powerful—so much so that Grandpa took up the task of writing his biography.

My father, Philip E. Howard Jr., the elder of two sons, proposed to Katharine Gillingham in 1920 and married her in 1922. I see that FATHER AND SON was published in 1922, the author no doubt having been galvanized to put down on paper important things he would want his son to know in case he became a father. That event took place on December 9, 1923, when Philip Gillingham Howard was born in Brussels, Belgium, where our parents were missionaries. Grandpa's book, FATHER AND SON, is a revelation to me — I had given little thought to my father's relationship to his father, but a glance at the table of contents is a compendium of essential matters, many of which may hardly have been thought of by most fathers today. Page after page causes me to say, "My father learned that." As a young missionary assigned to children's work, he did not neglect the first years of his own son's upbringing. I remember the old black-and-white framed photo of him with his binoculars around his neck, holding the hand of his two-year-old, somewhere on a sand dune by the North Sea. He taught all of us to read books— good, worthwhile books (some of them humorous, some suitably spiritual, many classics and, of course, missionary biographies). He and Mother saw to it that we were exposed to many men and women of God in the flesh, a large number of them missionaries who sat at our dinner table and whose tales riveted us.

My father's Christianity was of the seven-day-a-week sort. He rose early in order to have time alone with God before we came to breakfast. After breakfast there were always family prayers, which began with a hymn (all stanzas), followed by Bible reading, then prayer on our knees, ending in unison with The Lord's Prayer. After dinner, we were not excused until Daddy had read a portion of Daily Light, a little book of pure scripture selections for morning and evening. Again he prayed.

He helped with schoolwork and took an interest in our teachers. I was thrilled when my sixth-grade public school teacher accepted an invitation to dinner—she had been to *China*, had actually ridden in a ginrickshaw, and Daddy drew her out with many questions for our benefit, as he did with all guests. He took us to the office of **The Sunday School Times** (where he was first the associate editor and later the editor) and loved to trot us all around and introduce us to the secretaries, receptionist, and the linotype operators. We knew about his work. When we left the nest, one became a home missionary and pastor, another an academic professor, and four of us foreign missionaries. Our parents counseled us, prayed for us, and *let go*—remaining, however, keenly interested in our chosen fields.

When the six of us get together, which is seldom, we sing hymns (in parts), we laugh a lot and—probably more than anything else—we talk about our amazing parents. Of course we saw nothing amazing about them at all when we were growing up. But what a heritage they left, and what a responsibility is laid on us who are now grandparents to *lift high the cross*. God help us to help the fathers, first by prayer, by cheerful and loving encouragement, and then—only if asked—by advice.

Elisabeth Elliot
June 1998

I

PREPARING FOR FATHERHOOD

SHALL we talk together very plainly about it? Men get so completely absorbed in the imperatives of the day's work that a good deal goes unthought and unsaid among us that should come out into the open of conversation much more often than is our habit. What is it to be a father, anyway? What is the father's real place in the home, especially in his relation to that boy of his? What is a father for—to support the family and to chip in an occasional hint on management, and to stand as a square-shouldered, competent buffer between this rude, jostling world and that group at home? All of this, indeed. But what more? Every man of us knows there is a lot more to fatherhood than that; yet how easy it is to become hazy as to the fine points of this wonderful task and privilege of fathering!

For example, how much thorough and conscious preparation does a young man usually undertake in order to be all that a father ought to be? Years to become a good engineer, chemist, doctor, teacher, preacher, he will spend in elaborate and costly toil and patient sacrifice. But come now, honestly—how many of us have especially studied the best that can be found on how to be a real father?

Some of us can look back far enough now to wonder with a shiver how we ever had the nerve to undertake family

1

duties when we were so little prepared for the fathering we now see should have been done so much better than we ever managed to do it. And if any of us has a bit of experience to recount that might help some other father, a lesson learned in the school of home life, especially as touching "that boy," let's talk it over!

Just how can a man prepare for the high calling of fatherhood? Would you agree that the following are some of the ways, some of the considerations he ought to face?

He must begin young. Very young. So young that when he has boys of his own he can enter with keen sympathy into their boyhood problems, through vivid memory of what such days meant to him when he looked far ahead and resolved to create no possible hereditary handicaps for the boys that might be his. And if any man of us did not begin as young as he now wishes he had, let him begin now, and be grateful that our God so often most lovingly breaks through heredity, smashes its cold theories, and sends his mercy like a cleansing stream sweeping away what we feared might be passed on to the boy who is dearer to us than life. Do you remember that encouraging word of Thomas Fuller's, a chaplain of Oliver Cromwell's time? It's a good passage for a father in all humility and gratitude to tuck away in his memory treasures:

> "Lord, I find the genealogy of my Saviour strangely checkered with four remarkable changes in four immediate generations. (1) Rehoboam begat Abijah; that is, a bad father begat a bad son. (2) Abijah begat Asa; that is, a bad father a good son. (3) Asa begat Jehoshaphat; that is, a good father a good son. (4) Jehoshaphat begat Joram; that is, a

good father a bad son. I see, Lord, from hence that my father's piety cannot be entailed; that is bad news for me. But I see also that actual impiety is not always hereditary; that is good news for my son."

Good news, indeed, for every man as he looks into the clear eyes of his boy and resolves anew, in Christ's strength and grace to prepare *now* as never before, perhaps, for right fathering.

He must allow a large section of time in his life program for fatherhood. It takes time. It cannot fairly be allotted the fag ends of physical and mental vigor. To make a fair allotment requires sound thinking in advance, no a catch-as-catch-can wrestling bout with strong-armed demands upon time after the boy is really yours. In one home where there are two little boys, one of three and the other less than two years of age, the father, a young man of twenty-six, in charge of a growing and very engrossing business, takes time to tell the little chaps their good-night stories, and to read aloud to the busy mother chapters from Henry Clay Trumbull's "Hints on Child Training." And his face lighted up with the keenest interest as he told a visitor about the twenty-five books on child training he had already gathered. He has given time to choosing and arranging just the right pictures for the nursery; he gives time to the little boys themselves. He is in training as a father, and because he knows this, he so arranges his days that he is not forever saying, "Ask mother about that," but he takes the time in which he can gladly say to the small boys, "Come to father now, and we'll have a story." It is all allowed for in his day.

3

Another father, admittedly one of the busiest men of our time, a man of world-wide interests, great productivity in the writing of important books, and away from home in public work about half his time, has for years made it his rule to take one Sunday a month out of his crowded schedule of addresses to devote to his home, in family fellowship and family attendance upon the services of the Church. And on all his weekday home evenings, a certain time after dinner is carefully set apart before he goes to his study as the children's own time. It is theirs, and father is theirs absolutely, with no distractions of lesser importance, such as books waiting to be written.

One of our ablest American lawyers, and a leader as well in the affairs of his denomination and city and state, has made it his custom to decline ordinarily to make addresses on Sunday that would take him away from home, because he has set apart on that day for his children the free hours between church services. Then they have the right of way. Their claims are held inviolate and sacred. A regular time—of course plus other special times—is in this busy man's program as belonging to his children. If you are a young man, perhaps not married, or in the first year or two of married life, are you holding in sufficient prominence among your allotments of time the preparation for and the duties of fatherhood in the home itself?

He should get clear and act uncompromisingly on the foundations of personal faith in Christ, so that he will have his own footing on solid ground and be well able to lead the boy securely and satisfyingly. That means Bible study; a clear stand for Christ; membership in a church; and well-defined

4

reasons for the faith that he holds. The father who is not a believing Christian, working at the job, is furnishing a very murky and miasmatic atmosphere for his boy at home. No man, whether he is considering the problems of fatherhood or not, should be hazy or non-committal here. And as a father, how can a man hope to have the wisdom, the patience, the self-sacrificing devotion, the pure objectives, and the sound counsel that he would give to his boy, if he is willing himself to be uncertain as to Christ, and—yes, let's put it bluntly— unsaved? So let a man not simply because of his own salvation get clear and act unequivocally on his relation to Christ but let him be fully assured that he is crippled in advance as a father if he doesn't know what he ought to know about Christ, and doesn't do what he ought to do to make his testimony for Christ valid and effective. There's no use in blinking the issue. All the good technical books in child-study and psychology of varied application, and all one's experience in practical dealings with the boys in the home, come short of their usefulness as guides to better fatherhood if the father is simply groping along in a religious fog. "How does your father look at these questions?" was asked of a boy who was discussing with an older friend the boy's religious convictions, which were very hazy. "Well, I don't exactly know," the boy replied. "Lately he has got hold of something or other, something new, I guess—New Thought, maybe, but not just that— and he doesn't say much, but reads a lot, and seems to have something or other, but I don't know what." Do you wonder that the boy is groping, too? Have you considered what it means to a growing boy to be certain chiefly of one thing in his religious thinking, and that is that his father has "something or other," but he doesn't know what?

This is just now a particularly confusing time, religiously, for the boy. Conflicting voices reach him from every side. And it is a time of confusion for fathers, younger and older. Subtle processes are at work underneath the outward fabric of church and home such as have had time in other lands to work out their reactions in religious indifference, moral declension, and agnosticism. Some of us who have sons, some of us who are only on the threshold of fatherhood, would do well to re-investigate the grounds of our faith by fresh and prayerful study of the Scriptures, and by reading over again such a book as Bushnell's "The Character of Jesus Forbids His Possible Classification with Men," or Robert E. Speer's "The Deity of Christ," or C. G. Trumbull's "What Is the Gospel?" or Dr. W. H. Griffith Thomas' "Christianity Is Christ" —all of them brief, clear, illuminating, and invigorating to faith. Preparation for fatherhood demands well-informed, clean-cut, and plainly definable conclusions on the person of Christ, the true integrity of the Scriptures, and the complete adequacy of the Gospel for the needs of today. For the boy will very early ask questions, and rightly. Can you answer him straight from well-informed conviction, or are you to be in the position of that would-be wharf-side mission worker who knew little of nautical matters, of whom the water-front boys said: "Yes, he talked to us about two things he knew nothin' about—ships and religion." Will you need to be always referring your boy to some other boy's father when he asks why folks believe the Bible, and how we know we are right when we put the Christian religion ahead of others? Prepare! And allow time for getting many of these inevitable questions well cleared up in your own mind before that live bundle of eager questioning is yours!

He must prepare to keep young. That means deliberate planning, too. As sure as you live, even though now you may be only a year or two out of college or training school, the interest you have in track and field, in diamond and gridiron, in swim and hike and the glow of a camp fire will not survive the pressure of business and professional cares, unless you keep up and keep on in some of these blessedly refreshing things. Some day if you are not on your guard, you will get too busy, or too tired, or too lazy to do any more than talk like a "has-been," and show the boys your medals. But hold on to your ability and interest in some of these things, so that you can let your boys know you are with them for all you are worth.

My father used to take me hunting with him when I was so small that he would give me a lift by carrying me on his gun-case, where I stood with one foot on either side of his hand, and holding with both my hands to his shoulder. In his practice as a country physician then he used to take me on long rides, telling me about his work and showing me some of his surgical results. He taught me to manage horses and to ride when I was eight; took me on an Adirondack deer hunt when I was fifteen, and was more elated than I when I got a buck; boxed with me and gave me all I wanted when he was fifty and I was a college boy. And now that it is my turn, do you mind if I say that it seems to me that I still ought to be preparing for a fatherhood that I greatly desire should increasingly mean something to my two college boys—and the girls, too!—by work and play with them on their own terms?

Some of my friends may think that I ought to be more dignified, but I frankly confess that I do not look with shame upon a snap-shot of my biggest boy and his father doing a hand-stand side by side on a country road with their heels up against a barn door. Parenthetically, I'll admit that I'm glad it was a snapshot, and not a time exposure! It seems to me that a father ought most surely to carry the genuineness, the enthusiasm, the aliveness, the wholesome beginnings of an all-round, well-developed boyhood clean over into his life with his own boys. We'll talk further about this, in concrete ways, as our conversations continue.

But man! For the boy's sake, keep your boyhood alive, so that you can be a boy worth your boys not in any artificial way, not as a concession, but because you and he belong together.

It will not be regarded as a departure from the limitations of these studies of father, home, and boy if the suggestion is here made that right preparation for fatherhood requires the developing of a sense of partnership with Motherhood. For was not Longfellow right when he wrote:

"As unto the bow the cord is,
So unto the man is woman;
Though she bends him, she obeys him,
Though she draws him, yet she follows-
Useless each without the other!"

Not as the task or privilege of an individual in solitary responsibility are we to regard fatherhood, but every man who looks forward to, or now has, a father's opportunities ought to bear fully in mind that he has a partner in Motherhood. That is a very heartening fact to the right-minded man. He will not allow a foreshortened view of fatherhood to cramp his sense of absolute personal responsibility for his boy's training, nor, on the other hand, will he fail to recognize that he is not alone in the task, but that there is one with whom he must learn to work in partnership, and whose share in the enterprise is very large—larger than his by far, in point of time spent in direct service and costly self-sacrifice. The father must from the beginning prepare, not for an arbitrary individualism in enforcing his convictions on child training, irrespective of the mother's counsel, but for a sane, ready, patient co-operation, with a full knowledge of the material in which he is working.

This means modesty of opinion, openness of mind, teachability, and tact in putting his resources at the disposal of the family—not mere money, but himself—and a sensible recognition of the fact that a measure is not necessarily right and wise simply because he says it is.

Children—boys in particular—are very keen to notice when father and mother are not pulling together. And the father will not find co-operation a ready-made garment that can be slipped on at will, like a house coat, after the boy is a member of the family. In his perspective of marriage itself, in his ideal of womanhood, in his vision of a real home, a man needs to perceive that the whole beautiful arrangement is a true partnership, a glad adjustment of life to the life of another, a rich opportunity to be a friend.

It is idle to suppose that a home can be anything more than a house without that very spirit and practise of partnership. But this does not just happen along, tramp-fashion. Most men are too individualistic, too pre-occupied with the drive of ambition, the concentration of energy upon productive or executive or research faculties, to come sufficiently into partnership with motherhood. Far too much responsibility is shifted to the mother. A man ought to keep himself aware of this tendency as he faces toward fatherhood, and as he values the sanctities of the marriage bond and appreciates the significance of fatherhood, he ought to plan definitely for more than his share of the partnership in child-training. Taking the long look ahead, what, after all, is he to stand for as a member of that family group? He must decide—the earlier the better. It would be worth far more than any cost a man can put into it to have such an influence, such a blending of partnership ideals and service as that described by Elizabeth Harrison in "A Study of Child Nature," when she writes: "It has been one of the great privileges of my life to have had entrance to an almost ideal home, where husband and wife were filled with the most exalted love I have ever known. In time the husband was called hence. The wife said: 'All that was beautiful and attractive in my life went out with my husband, and yet I know that I must, for the very love I bear him, remain and rear our child as he would have him reared.'"

Do you see how the strong and loving soul of a man who evidently had taken his fatherhood seriously was still sharing, by support and remembered counsel, in the partnership for the sake of the boy? Would the preparation for, and practise of fatherhood, as represented by most of us, survive such a test as that?

II

THE FIRST FEW YEARS

He was a very little fellow, sitting up in his crib in the children's ward. When I came to him on my visit he seemed more eager to talk than any of the other little boys in the room. He had heard me chatting with the others from crib to crib, and when I stood beside him he looked up, his lips trembled, and he pulled one leg out from under the bed-clothes.

"I've got a sore leg," he explained (he had indeed!), "and I'm goin' to have a operation today—yes, sir, today!"

I took a good look at the infected leg, and then with the cheeriest smile I could muster, I said, "Well, youngster, you'll be glad to feel better, won't you, and you won't know anything about that operation while the doctor is doing it. Anybody here with you?"

The tears came into his eyes. "No, sir," he replied, "nobody here. I haven't any mother."

"But what about father?" I asked, expectantly.

"Father can't be here," answered the little chap. "He's goin' huntin' today."

When he said, "Father can't be here," there flashed upon my mind the vision of a hard-working man held by his task—but *"goin' huntin'!"* I did what I could to cheer the almost baby boy, and I was not entirely free from the earnest desire to do a little "huntin'" on my own account that day, and waylay that father for a few moments' conversation.

The circumstances make this seem like an extreme case of irresponsible fatherhood; yet it is not as rare as it ought

11

to be. For it is much too easy for fatherhood to stand aside from the fellowship, the shared life of the very small boy, and, on various theories of action, to let some one else have both the privilege and the burden.

The man who visualizes clearly, and measures his fatherhood unselfishly will not leave out of his program of responsibility the first years of his child's life. The man will have a hard time in the other years of his under-graduate and postgraduate course in fatherhood, who skips or fumbles this freshman period.

It is all very well for a man to have the honest conviction that the boy's mother can do many things for the boy much better than the father can. But she ought not to be asked by the father to be both mother and father in the beginning years, or at any time during their life together. There are men who not only have seen this obligation clearly, but who have acted upon it so consistently that their example is a challenge to Christian chivalry and unselfishness and sense of responsibility. Do you recall that passage in "John Halifax": "A child—little feet to go pattering about our house . . . a little voice to say 'Father.' You cannot think what an awful joy it is to be looking forward to a child: a little soul of God's giving, to be made fit for his eternity." And if you will link with this joyous and solemnizing forward look, Carlyle's retrospect, "The history of a man's childhood is the description of his parents [not mother alone] and environment," you will find the two meeting like rays of white light upon the duty of a realized and fully accepted fatherhood in the beginning years.

The prolonged infancy of the child is the father's call and opportunity for a lasting ministry. To postpone his fellowship with his boy until the "companionable" age is to miss the mark. No father can fully understand the little fellow whose life is unfolding before his eyes if he regards him simply as a very precious but highly mysterious, and perhaps explosive, possession that somehow belongs to him, but is the care of someone else.

The father will be too small or too busy to interest the big boy if he counts himself too big or too busy to be interested in the little boy.

"Man in the savage state," writes Westermarck, "is generally supposed to be rather indifferent to the welfare of his wife and children, and this is really often the case, especially if he be compared with civilized man." But he quotes Macdonald's "Africana" to the effect that in some African tribes "a father has to fast after the birth of a child, or take some such method of showing that he recognizes that he as well as the mother should take care of the young stranger." At the other extreme of civilization, in a highly organized society, and with enormous demands upon his time and strength, and burdened with world-responsibilities, was the heartening spectacle of a great leader's fellowship with his children, when evening after evening a President of the United States read and romped with his small boys. Who can read "Theodore Roosevelt's Letters to His Children" without devoutly wishing that more fathers would take the time as he did, not only to write chummy letters, sometimes dictated from the barber's chair, to the big boys at school and college, but to play, yes, just *play*—with the youngest, in the nursery? Are we too busy? Roosevelt was no idler. Have we more important work to do than to chum with the small boy? Roosevelt had fairly important work on hand, too! Our difficulty is, in part, that as fathers we get the minor and the major tasks reversed in importance.

Do you know that keen little story of Laura E. Richards, in her fascinating book, "The Golden Windows"? She calls it "A Matter of Importance." The Angel-Who-Attends-to-Things was hastening along when a Duke called to him to consult him about the succession to the dukedom. "I cannot attend to you this morning," said the Angel, "I am engaged on business of importance." And he went on.

As he passed by a Bishop's palace, the Bishop called to him to consult him about the Great Synod. The Angel shook his head.

"I am on business of importance," he said, "I cannot attend to trifles this morning."

Soon he passed by a King's palace, and the King summoned him to advise concerning an impending attack from the enemy.

"By and by," said the Angel. "I am on business of importance now, and cannot stop for trifles." And he hurried on.

The Duke, the Bishop, and the King followed him to see what such an important matter could be—followed him into a dingy court, where a little child stood crying as if his heart would break.

The Angel gathered the child in his arms. "Hush, hush," he cried. "It is all right, dear. You took the wrong turning, that was all. She is just around the corner."

And the child's mother ran to the little group and gathered the child into her arms. The Angel rose up and looked around at the Duke, the Bishop, and the King. "Are *you*, there?" he said. "Now I can attend to your little matters."

Unless the father recognizes that the prolonged infancy of his child is very rich in these "matters of importance" he will have no adequate conception of what has occurred from month to month, and what can be brought to pass, in the life of the little one for whom he has so great a responsibility. Whence does the little child derive his idea of God? He is soon told by some one that God is his Heavenly Father; but what idea of God does the word "father" convey to him?

Do you agree with S. D. Gordon in his "Quiet Talks on Home Ideals" when he says: "Father and mother are as God to the child. That is to say, they are to the child in the place of God, until the child's awakening thought can be transferred to his parents' God, and then find out how much more God is than they; and yet simply 'more,' not different in kind. We are telling him by our lives what God is—if we are; maybe what He isn't. Whatever we are telling with presence and life, that God is, in the child's thought."

It is in the life of the very little child that the thought of God as a father so readily finds its place and influence. A man may think that the mother, in her tenderness and faithfulness and loving care, will sufficiently verify by her life and words the thought of God's heavenly care, and that the father may wisely be a sympathetic onlooker, rather than a constant participant in the details of the picture of a Heavenly Father that is taking shape in the child's soul. But the father cannot avoid this even if he would. Far better is it for him to recognize the mothering duty that is his own, from the beginning, and to enter into the significance of the profound truth back of Mr. Gordon's story of a man who came to understand what fatherhood can mean.

"A minister," writes Mr. Gordon, "was preaching to his home congregation on Sabbath morning. His son five years old sat in the minister's family pew, with others there. The strain of life had been too much for the mother's strength; the tether of life had worn thin, and raveled out, and then parted, and she had slipped away. It was said, in an undertone, among the families of the church that the father of the boy, broken-hearted over his loss, ministered with his own hands to the little fellow's needs, doing what a mother's hands commonly do.

"He was preaching as usual this Sabbath morning, and in his sermon spoke of a mother's care, and said, 'Who can take the place of a mother?' His little son, listening intently, spoke out, with the unconscious artlessness of a child, and with the slow speech and the thin treble of childish lips, that could be distinctly heard in the quiet of the church, he said, 'I think a father does very well.' A sudden hush cast its soft spell over the church, as the father swallowed something in his throat, and with glistening eyes smiled bravely down into his little son's face, and then went quietly on with his sermon."

For the fatherhood of God includes motherhood, and no father can rightly exclude from his own fatherhood the mothering that the true father gives to his little child.

"Every parent," writes President Thwing in his historical and social study, "The Family," "who dares to take upon himself the awful responsibility of calling a human life into being, who places himself in God's hands as the instrument of divine creative power, assumes a trust which should exclude every form of selfishness. Beyond the right of being well-born, every child has the right to the best training his parents can give. He has the right to the personal care of both father and mother, a care which can never be delegated to others without serious loss to both parent and child."

It is a part of the holy intimacy of father and child that the father should learn very early the difference between doing things for, and living with, his boy. The little child is no less sensitive to the difference in the two attitudes than is the older child. His awakening awareness of the world about him seeks a sympathetic sharing of his thrilling experiences. Thus a little boy playing in a western room late one afternoon caught a glimpse of the wonderful autumn sunset through the trees. He stood erect, and then rushing to the window, clambered up to a better point of view on the window seat, and excitedly called to his father, "Come, see, see!" pointing vigorously to the glow that had arrested his dawning appreciation of the beautiful. The father hurried to the little fellow's side, and shared his eagerness as together they saw the boy's first keenly realized sunset. Did this incident have any part in that boy's steadily increasing and intelligent love of nature as the years have brought him into many glad experiences of the out-of-doors?

A father learned a lesson in sharing, when watching one of his small boys busily at work with building blocks. From his armchair the man ventured one or two off-hand architectural suggestions, whereupon the little chap remarked wistfully, "I like it better when you play on the floor with me." On the floor it was the next instant; and on the floor of the boy's unfolding experiences, with the boy, not towering above him, that father says that it has been since then his desire and purpose to live.

Living with the small boy involves many responsibilities and privileges that a more remote and magisterial attitude never knows. A man soon realizes how imitative a little boy can be, if he is with his boy enough to make observations. Intimacy increases imitativeness, and hence a high degree of responsibility on the man's part for every habit, every peculiarity, good or otherwise, of his own. A New England farmer who very late in life became a father was greatly taken with that baby boy of his. Almost as soon as the baby could talk and walk he swore as innocently and as naturally as he asked for food. The father was genuinely distressed. He was a profane man himself, but he did not wish his boy to be like him in this. "I don't know," he complained in the boy's very presence, "where that boy gets them cuss words. I keep him with me most o' the time, and when he's around I never say a thing o' that kind." What was the real trouble with that father? What is the difficulty with the man who passes on to his imitative little child a habit that he himself deplores? He cannot help passing on in some degree *what he is, and what he has,* in the intimacy of father and son. Because this is so, it is a heartening fact that the small child is sensitively imitative, too, in the direction of a father's forthshowing, conscious or unconscious, of habits that help. In very simple illustration of this is the case of two little boys whose room at night was usually littered with the youngsters' garments after the flight to slumberland. Orders and warnings did not seem to amount to much. What would really help the little fellows? Their father had a place where he could hang his own clothes at night, but the boys had none that invited order at all. So the father fastened two good strong clothing hooks on a door inside the boys' room, showed just how the clothes should be hung there, and made it a point to appreciate the careful way in which the clothes thereafter were regularly, and with pride, hung exactly there. The little boys could now be as orderly as any one and they were. And did the father have to be careful, too? He did; and he has to now, or be in disgrace!

What tractable, eager, wide-eyed little chaps they are, after all, those baby boys of whom Mary Lamb wrote:

> "Thou straggler into loving arms,
> Young climber-up of knees,
> When I forget thy thousand ways
> Then life and all shall cease!"

And what memories—what generous and glowing and pervading memories *they* have of us fathers! They remember the best about us, to their joy—and to our shame that there was not more of the best to remember. They are learners, but what heaven-sent teachers they are! How rude and wintry is our manhood, when untouched by the melting sunshine of the new life given into the keeping of our fatherhood! Do you know that poem from a loving father-heart, Patterson Du Bois's "Fatherhood"?

> "My baby boy, I sing of thee
> Because thou art like song to me.
> Thy joys and fears, thy smiles and tears,
> Are rhythmic in their rising;
> Thy pantomimes, like tropes and rhymes,
> Are full of sweet surprising.
> A little lyric bit thou art;

A drama quickens in thy heart,
Concealed forsooth;
But through thy deep soul-magic
I see the truth—
Thy comedies are tragic.

"Thou atom of the ages,
Thou force among the forces
Out from the Source of sources,
Thou puzzler of the sages,
Back comes to me thy mimicry;
This heart of mine beats on in thine,
One life divine—-
Thy destiny
In me."

It is in the interpretation of the divine life, the memory of the Godward leadings, the tenderness of an overshadowing, guarding love that fatherhood has such a marvelous privilege in living with the little child. No father can safely or rightly stand apart from those earliest years of intimacy with his little boy. How much the boy expects of you! How utterly right you seem to him! Are you responding in tenderness and strength and ready sympathy, and understanding? Let's not blink these questions, or others like them.

Are you exhibiting normally in your home by the household habits on week day and on Sunday the fact that you do put God first in your planning and doings, so that what you say about Him, and the Lord Christ, may not be on the other side of the chasm separating what you say from what you do? That little boy of yours knows so well when he is living in a real fatherhood! Will you listen to the testimony of a man, far along in years when he wrote the words, but who had not forgotten? It is a joy beyond words to remember that a father can create memories like this for his boy:

"A sensitive, timid little boy, long years ago, was accustomed to lie down to sleep in a low 'trundle-bed,' which was rolled under his parents' bed by day, and was brought out for his use by night. As he lay there by himself in the darkness, he could hear the voices of his parents, in their lighted sitting-room, across the hallway, on the other side of the house. It seemed to him that his parents never slept; for he left them awake when he was put to bed at night, and he found them awake when he left his bed in the morning. So far this thought was a cause of cheer to him, as his mind was busy with imaginings in the weird darkness of his lonely room.

"After loving good-night words and kisses had been given him by both his parents, and he had nestled down to rest, this little boy was accustomed, night after night, to rouse up once more, and to call out from his trundle-bed to his strong-armed father, in the room from which the light gleamed out, beyond the shadowy hall-way, 'Are you there, papa?' And the answer would come back cheerily, 'Yes, my child, I am here.' 'You'll take care of me tonight, papa; won't you?' was then his question. 'Yes, I'll take care of you, my child,' was the comforting response. 'Go to sleep now. Good-night.' And the little fellow would fall asleep restfully, in the thought of those assuring good-night words.

"A little matter that was to the loving father; but it was a great matter to the sensitive son. It helped to shape the son's life. It gave the father an added hold on him; and it opened up the way for his clearer understanding of his dependence on the loving watchfulness of the All-Father. And to this day when that son, himself a father and a grandfather, lies down to sleep at night, he is accustomed, out of the memories of that lesson of long ago, to look up through the shadows of his earthly sleeping-place into the far-off light of his Father's presence, and to call out, in the same spirit of childlike trust and helplessness as so long ago, 'Father, you'll take care of me tonight; won't you?' And he hears the assuring answer come back, 'He that keepeth thee will not slumber. The Lord shall keep thee from all evil. He shall keep thy soul. Sleep, my child, in peace.' And so he realizes the twofold blessing of a father's good-night words."[1]

[1] From "Hints on Child Training," by H. Cay Trumbull.

III

WHEN HE JOINS "THE BUNCH"

ONCE it was "the gang"; now it is mostly "the bunch." Thus language changes, but the thing itself, that inevitable institution of boyhood, changes not at all. For the gang, or the bunch, persists, whether the boys wear linen collars and bare knees or collarless shirts and bare feet. The same old mysterious cohesion brings the bunch into being.

It was so up in that New England town where a boy from one of the homes under the elms belonged to a bunch made up in part of boys from the tenements. A boy was a boy to him, if he liked him, and it wasn't kinship in cash that explained the bunch, but kinship in spirit. So one night, when an itinerant "variety" show came to town, the father of the tenement boy who was just then best liked by the elm-shaded boy was the escort of the two in attending the show. But it was a doomed scheme. As the three stood in the jam outside the town hall door, the dusky face of a Negro coachman was seen peering through the crowd, and without ceremony Dave, the boy from the good street, of course under active protest, was led out of the crowd and straight home.

Why? he demanded to know. Well, it wasn't the place for him down there with that crowd. But wasn't Gene there and wasn't Gene's *father* there, and so everything must be all right! Gene was all right, and of course, it followed that his father must be doubly right for fathers must be so, anyway. Thus reasoned the eight-year-old member of the bunch in which Gene of the tenements was his chum. But that show had to proceed without the small boy, who was taken home. Somehow, he couldn't see through the thing then.

There was another in the bunch for whom Dave cared just about as much as he did for Gene—one Charlie by name. Of course Gene was a little more interesting because he was a Canuck, and lived in a part of the town that was somewhat exciting. But Charlie was all right. He and Dave were fellow-sufferers at the cruel hands of an arithmetic teacher who, strangely enough, wanted correct answers to "sums." Both boys had somehow managed to pass a very severe examination (exams always are severe!) in the dreaded subject, and each was trying to find out how the other had managed to accomplish the feat. After much shuffling and hesitancy, Charlie at last confessed that he had *prayed* about his exam, and in that way had passed. Dave had not known that side of his chum, but he well knew what Charlie meant. He was silent. Charlie had intimated that he was afraid Dave might laugh at him if he told how that exam was managed. But Dave did not laugh. The two small boys of eight or nine, strolling along the shaded street, were already feeling their way into the great issues of life.

Within the same gang, then, were boys who meant quite different things to Dave. They were not seen much in his home. They met mostly at school, on the streets, usually in an incidental, touch-and-go fashion, and sometimes in a clash with a tough bunch that tried to terrorize the town; sometimes playing circus, or Indian, or walking on stilts, or coasting on the glare crust of snow on the steep Vermont hillsides. How much did Dave's father know about the bunch—about Gene on the one hand, and Charlie on the other? And how much of the home training, the home atmosphere, would go with Dave when, with a shout, he would "beat it" out of the front gate and down the street, in answer to the beckonings of the bunch in the distance? Eight years old, and even then an enthusiastic member of a social group outside the home!

And that is the law. The outer contacts are inevitable. Dave cannot, should not, indeed, live on the inside of the front gate. Your problem as a father is not how to stave off as long as possible the schooling he gets, and gives, in his own boyhood social groups, but how to guide it and convert it into useful material for his total development.

There is hardly a greater general problem of fatherhood as related to the boy in the years just preceding the teens than the entrance of these collateral influences into the boy's life. For in one sense they are beyond parental advance control. That is to say, they come like gusts of wind on an inland lake, from any and all directions, and not in accordance with the prevailing wind. Outside the home every boy is exposed to these collateral, extra-parental influences of his bunch, and to many other influences besides. He may pick up a magazine in the home of a chum, and in two minutes get mentally mired in bogs the very existence of which was unknown to him. Even in the moment of writing these words a man in middle life entered the library where I am at work, and we greeted each other as old friends. I am startled as I recall a talk we had when we were small boys (he was a son of the manse—a boy of unusual ability) in which he broken-heartedly told me of the persistent attempts of one of the bunch in our city street to break down his boyhood purity, and I remember, as of yesterday, the distress in his voice as he confided in me,

25

his chum. He passed through the tempest of boyhood by the grace of God, into a life of usefulness in business and in the Church, but it was true that in those days his home knew nothing of his testing times. His father? Well, his father was not living then. But if he had been—come now, how many of us as fathers really are alive, really *know what are the influences* for good or for evil that are flowing about our boys outside the home? We cannot always forestall them, or manipulate them to our liking, but we can at least know them, and help the boy to see them level-eyed.

We must find out what these influences are by quiet observation more than by close questioning. Sometimes too much questioning gives rise in the small boy's heart to the suspicion that his father does not really trust him. And if a boy comes under the sinister spell of that notion, then there is a barrier at once thrown up between himself and his father.

Much can be learned if the father will be at home some evening when his boy has a chum or two up in his room. He is proud of that room. His treasures are there. While the boys are looking things over, the father can drop in and cheerfully look the boys over, enter into their talk, tell them a story—a *short* one!—that fits in with something of interest to them, and let them see that he hasn't forgotten when he was a boy. Any man who has been among boys at all, with his eyes open, and his heart warm toward them, can make keen deductions from a bit of fellowship with his boy's chums.

An overnight in the open with the youngsters helps wonderfully to let a father get what the boys might call "inside dope." Some of the bunch come to the house in the late afternoon, and pack the haversacks. Father, in old clothes, shoulders his haversack and blanket, while the little fellows trudge along with their outfit, as they make their way through the town and over the hill, and along the creek to the woods where there is a grassy ravine and a spring of good water.

Then come the delights of making camp, father *not* bossing the job, but pitching right in as a hewer of wood and drawer of water, and cooker of bacon, plus anything else that he ought to be. After supper, as the twilight falls and the night wind begins to whisper in the hemlocks, the camp fire crackles, the little chaps gather round it for a talk and a sing, and father is just a boy with them, chipping in with the rest in the talk, but not swamping the youngsters with his mighty store of wisdom! A good-night prayer together by and by seems to come in just right, and then the campers crawl into their shelter tents, and presently their chatter dies away, and sleep is upon them.

But father doesn't sleep at first. He is looking out at the stars above the hemlocks, listening to the wind in the trees, the breathing of the boys around him, and picturing to himself just who and what these little fellows are, his boy's chums. And he wonders not only what they mean to his boy, but how his boy is influencing them. In that brief evening he has seen how quickly one boy leaps to wash dishes; how another never knows where anything is; how another neatly avoids doing what he can switch over to any one else to do. A little world of educational influences, as complex as the cosmic mind, is gathered around that miniature camp. It is very late when sleep comes to the man; very early when he emerges from the tent, and shows a "morning face," with a cheery word to the little fellows who tumble out ready for the new day. In that one night father has learned enough about his boy's "bunch" to give him a reason for saying a word now and then to his boy about things to look out for. No, the boys were not as free as if father had not been there; but it is a dull father indeed who cannot make safe deductions from his fellowship even for a little while with small boys— or big boys, either.

When the boy begins to show signs of belonging to a gang, or bunch, then *it is high time for the father to bestir himself and get counted in. He can be. He ought to be, not as a mentor, not as a guardian, but as a real chum.* In writing of some of the difficulties involved, Professor G. Walter Fiske has said:

> "The greater difficulty is the fact that the father, in growing older, has lost his youth, or rather his youthfulness. He has forgotten how it seemed to be a boy. The interests which absorbed him in his boyhood have been submerged in the colder tides of later life. The idealism, maybe, and the hero worship, and the noble altruism of adolescent days have been lost in the glare of life's realism. Perhaps the iconoclastic days have come, the saddest in human life. Imagination is dormant; memory is ineffective, dim, and fickle; boyish dreams and youthful visions are forgotten. And the *feelings,* the surest criterion of age, are greatly changed. The finer emotions and the naive enthusiasms, the man has lost forever; and with these his lost youth. It is one of the needless tragedies of life that men thus lose their youthful joy and the zest for living, and with it the real sympathy of their own boys.

What business has any boy's father a-growing old except in years and baldness—which don't count!"

It was probably with some such conception of his opportunity that a father, living in a suburban town, arranged to be out with his small boys in their rather elementary football practise whenever he could. Among other efforts to "belong," he would do his share by punting the ball clear over the high housetop from the front lawn to the rear. During one of these amazing exhibitions of football prowess, a small boy of the neighborhood bunch stood gazing awe-struck as he watched for the first time the lofty and successful flight of the ball. Then he strolled up to the man, and remarked, approvingly, "Well, I see you haven't lost the use of your kicker!" Had that acquaintance on the improvised gridiron anything to do with the willingness of that boy a few years later to confide in his football friend at a time of serious crisis? What father can know just how far some of his hours of fellowship with his boys and their chums will lead him in service to them Let him at least see to it that he *belongs.* If he does, not only his own boy but others will be the gainers, in so far as he is fulfilling the reasonable obligations of a true and righteous fatherhood.

Most boys are older than we think. Every father probably has had the experience of surprise over some unexpected revealing of his small boy's so-called precociousness. One almost hesitates to use that word because there are so many exceptions to the ordinary laws of the unfolding life. One does not usually suspect little fellows two or three years of age of being much interested in war news even before they are members of the bunch in the neighborhood. Hence a young father was quite taken aback one morning when out for a little walk with his two-year-old boy, as the child looked up at him and remarked, evidently as a comment upon the current news of the day, "Joubert is dead." The news had, indeed, just come from the Boer War about General Joubert's death, and the fact, caught somehow in table-talk, had impressed the little fellow enough to make that fact a part of his conversation. Thus the world-outlook may indeed begin almost before there is a neighborhood outlook.

The father of the small boy needs to take into account the forward look of the youngster and he need not be surprised at almost any sign of a maturing mind. Dr. Lilburn Merrill, in his altogether delightful and heart-searching book, "Winning the Boy," tells of an occasion upon which he and Judge Ben B. Lindsey were facing a turbulent, good-natured audience of boys. "Now up to this time," writes Dr. Merrill, "there was, as we thought, a port of entry to the good nature of every boy in the Union. And on this occasion we looked over the roomful of hopefuls and, being introduced, we as usual made a chummy salutation to 'de kids.' The kid spirit vanished with the salutation and the atmosphere became chilly. Then a black-headed Bohemian boy who was at least three years prematurely ensheathed in a pair of long trousers that reached from his armpits and left five inches of excess turned up at the bottom, spoke for the assembly: 'Gowan, what youse givin' us? You tink we is bleatin' nannies wid whiskers? We ain't kids, we's *guys!*'"

The promotion from the "kid" to the "guy" class is a very real thing, and a boy gets there much earlier than his father may suppose. One of my own small friends in the neighborhood, I have noticed of late, hardly ever speaks of the other fellows as anything but "guys." That word represents a horizontal section of the accumulated advance and upward growth of the boy who belongs to the bunch, for there is obviously a far greater distinction in being a "guy" than in being a "kid." To the preoccupied father the distinction may seem rather too fine for practical purposes, but, indeed, it is in his recognition of what such things mean to the boy, that he will find an intensifying of his fellowship with the boy.

In the very deepest things of the boy's life, this inner maturity that reveals itself in special ways will often cause the thoughtful father to stand by the bedside of his sleeping boy at night, or to kneel there, and ask God to give him, as a father, wisdom and sensitiveness enough to appreciate the little fellow who is teaching him so much. A little boy brought up in a family whose denominational affiliations had been strongly allied with the Baptist Church, but who had become members of a Presbyterian Church, yet without yielding their belief as to immersion, decided that he would like to join the Church. He was a clear-minded, energetic, out-of-doors little chap, full of fun and with a normal boy's interests in mechanics and games and stories. As the time drew near for him to make an open confession of his faith in Christ, he quietly told his parents without any hint from them that he wanted to be immersed. He said he had been thinking it all over and had made up his mind that immersion was the right way to be baptized. His parents respected the little fellow's decision and, with the entire concurrence of the Presbyterian pastor, the boy was baptized by immersion in a Baptist Church in the city from which his parents had come, and then was received into membership in the Presbyterian Church. To see that little fellow riding his wheel or playing football with the bunch, or adding his part to accentuate the noise of the neighborhood, one would little have guessed that the question of a mode of baptism would have been occupying his thought at all. But so it was; and so it is with other boys in ways that fathers least suspect, as the little fellows begin to find their footing on the threshold of the door that swings out from the home.

One reason why it is so needful to emphasize the often unexpected maturing of a little fellow's mind is found in the fact that fathers are so likely to plod along after the boy in the distant rear, without realizing that almost before they know it the youngster is advancing in ways which the father had not noticed. Mothers often perceive the real state of things long before fathers do, and this is not in accord with what should be the true balance of rightful parental partnership. Professor Fiske tells this story of a mother's discovery: "A certain wise mother, more discerning than her husband, discovered that her three small boys were slipping away from the home influence and spending much of their time elsewhere. They would do all their studying before supper, then hastily steal out for a long evening 'with the other boys.' They evaded her questions with unsatisfactory explanations. They began to grow pale and listless in appearance, did discreditable work at school, and became more and more unmanageable, until the mother was in despair. One night she followed the boys, and was appalled to find them with a few selected cronies in the back of a neighboring saloon, listening to the exciting stories of a maudlin old soldier, who shared with them his beer in return for their pocket-money. Prompt action and subsequent tactfulness saved the boys."

When the small boy begins to run with the bunch, the father must become a member, too. If that father is the right sort of "guy" he will be welcome. Oh, no; he doesn't need to be always there when anything is on, but he mustn't just glance around the corner of his newspaper when little Bill is "busting" to tell him about a great thing the bunch did, or plans to do, but he must put that paper clear down, and really care to listen to all that Bill wants to say. Bunch or no bunch, little Bill is always glad to have a home base, from which his excursions start, and to which he can come back without getting snubbed or chilled. And the pull of that home, when the father is his ever-ready, sympathizing chum, will greatly contribute to correct any of the undesirable temporary allurements of the mixed influence beyond the gate.

Father & Son

IV

HIS BOOKSHELF

IT IS his group of intimate friends—that row of books on the shelf which perhaps the boy himself built. And these books are building him. They have access to him when he is most impressionable, and they reach him in ways not always open to vocal counsel. A father not only ought to know what those books are saying to the boy, but he ought to have a hand in selecting what books shall companion his boy in the intimacy of friendship. For the relationship of book and boy is nothing less than that.

But how can a busy father help to get the right books into the hands of the right boy? And what are right books, after all, when "everybody" says a book is "strong" that you think is vile; and "everybody" says a book is "so true to life" that you think is just coarse; and "everybody" says a book is "so charmingly written" that you count mere twaddle? Then, too, where are you going to draw the line between letting the boy read what interests him most, and getting him to read what you think ought to interest him? Are you safe in turning him loose in the juvenile section of the public library, or even in the Sunday-school library—not only safe from coarseness and twaddle, but safe in letting him follow his reading bent at will, instead of leading him out into kinds of reading that you think will minister most to his future usefulness? The boy will read, just as he will be sure to have chums. As the boy goes pioneering in book-land, that alluring land of mysterious, glamorous vistas and beckoning buried treasure, can a busy father go just a step or two ahead? He can; and if he does not, then he can easily lose sight of the boy, and unhappily the boy will scarcely miss him in a land where the boy greatly needs an older chum who can see with a boy's eyes and explore with the eager spirit of youth.

We men do not read books enough. No, we are not really too busy. It is only that we do not use our time well. We spend a great deal of time in pointless conversation that might be spent in company with books, books that know how to say what we need to hear, books with the savor of salt in them, and not insipid and vapid like so much of the casual conversation at luncheon and on train and street-car. One of the busiest men of our time, engaged in exacting executive work, serving on many committees, with a world-wide correspondence, writer of many books, and a public speaker of international fame, ordinarily reads about eighty books each year. Yes, *reads* them, not by skimming through them, but by close, carefully annotated reading. The variety is wide—some are recent books, some the standard works that have weathered the years. But he reads in odd moments, on trains, on street-cars, between engagements, while waiting for appointments, catching time for a page or many pages, but planning to have a book with him wherever he goes.

Now note a simple incident. Would you call it a consequence? That man's thirteen-year-old boy was sailing with the family for Europe. The youngster was apparently seeing everything in the busy doings of the hour before the "all ashore" sounded. He would step to the rail, his quick eyes noting the activities on the wharfs and then back to a steamer chair he would go, and dropping down there, he would open wide a book he was holding and plunge into the pages for a few moments with the same eager interest he had shown in the dock-side doings. Oh, no, he wasn't your idea of a book-worm at all, but a vivid, energetic, all-round American lad whose father had been a great athlete and a star student — and a great reader in *the odd moments.* It will not do to dispose of the incident by calling it exceptional. The point is, do you read enough books, do you encourage your boy to read, in the time you could use if you would?

How much do you read aloud at home? Out from that simple and highly rewarding habit can come many a fine impulse for the boy to assemble a worthy company in his bookshelf. And even though you may not clearly trace specific results in the selecting of books by the boy himself, it is conceivable that in your reading aloud he may for the first time see as through an open window a little glimpse of the inviting land of books.

One father, a man of crowded days and many cares, but whose reading was wide and varied from his boyhood, used to read aloud to his only son, a live, imaginative, friendly, and fun loving boy. They had great times together. The boy was led into a love for books. He was the one among his school-fellows who had read more than any other. He did not claim this in the least It was only that when someone mentioned a really fine book for boys, he was nearly always likely to mention in his eager way something he had noticed in that very book. One evening during his early teens the fire-bells sounded out over the neighborhood. "Everybody" turned out. The next day one of his friends asked, "Were you at the fire last night?"

"Why, no," he answered. "I didn't go. Father and I were reading David Copperfield, and I didn't want to stop."

One moment! You think he ought to have dropped that book instantly? Well, some others have thought so, too. But this extreme case of a controlling interest in father-and-son reading is cited just because it is so extreme that it brings into sharp contrast the empty reading-life of many a father and son, who would have been on that evening not only unconcerned about books, but separated in their interests, and not even at home.

Reading aloud furnishes ideal opportunities for discovering what your boy lives, and enables you to arouse interest by comment, by your own appreciation, by elaborating a little on a reference, or by recalling to the boy's mind something he already knows. And by reading aloud from books in which the conversational or the narrative style is good, there is afforded a corrective of the all-too-careless and slovenly style of conversation so common among Americans. A father was reading to a missionary, whose field was in Japan, some selected passages from a modern translation of the New Testament. Neither noticed that a boy of five, a son of that home, was listening intently. He left the room quietly when the reading was finished, and going to his mother, he exclaimed, "Oh, Mother, that was the most wonderful reading I have ever heard!" The method was most ordinary; but what he had caught was not the method, but the words themselves as they reached his understanding in their fine yet somewhat colloquial simplicity. It was language that he understood because it was made up mostly of familiar words, and the sentences were not archaic, but of his own day. Do not misunderstand. I would not suggest the omission of reading aloud from the King James or the American Standard versions, for in those texts there is a language that we simply must not lose in these our changing times. But it is well also to let the Bible reach the hearing of the young by means of their own language—not in the slipshod, but in the choicest, English of our day.

Whether by reading aloud, or by the suggesting of good books, a father should, I believe, do certain definite services for the reading interests of his boy. He should:

1. Cultivate the boy's imagination, a faculty that often needs direction, and always is worth training, if for no other reason than for its foremost place in effective, constructive work in boyhood and manhood.

2. Equip the boy, from the time he begins to read, with real information about the common things around him.

3. Give him contact with noble lives through well told biographies, and in particular missionary biographies, than which there are none more appealing in heroism and in high accomplishment.

4. See to it that he becomes acquainted with good poetry, in accordance with his unfolding life—not the foolish fads of modern "free verse," but fine, vigorous, picturesque, and stirring verse, such, for example, as one finds in "Poems of Action," David Porter's excellent little collection of verse chiefly for boys.

5. Include in his reading, when the boy is still very young, some good Bible stories accurately and simply retold. As Ruskin has said, there is nothing more interesting to the

child than the Bible stories read from the Book itself. There are many religious books now that the growing boy will gladly read, as he begins to face boyhood's real problems, such as a number of the books by Robert E. Speer. Older boys especially would appreciate "Young Men Who Overcame," or "Servants of the King," or "A Young Man's Problems." Regular reading of the Bible day by day is a habit that can easily be started when the boy is very young, and continued by father and son alike. No reading whatever can take the place of this.

6. On the negative side, head off trash and worse by every method the father can adopt. Are you aware of the fact that among the best paying preparatory school advertising mediums of today—some say the best—are two magazines that are among the very worst in their moral influence? And why? Simply because they are read so extensively by the boys and girls of America whose parents can afford to send them to private schools, and these young readers so often take the initiative in selecting the schools they wish to attend. The father must guard the magazine table from the well-printed and alluring magazine degenerates that seem to be taken into so many homes with such easy tolerance and friendly welcome. And the bookshelf needs equally to be guarded, for many a book is well advertised by standard publishers that never should see the light at all—excepting the light of a bonfire.

Shall we glance here at a small bookcase in a certain boy's room and make a clinical examination of it? He is letting me look over his books as I sit at his desk. They have been gathered by him slowly, as his interests have unfolded; and they represent what he likes to have in his own room.

Will you look over the list with me, and note its range, its subjects, its deficiencies, and see what you would suggest by way of elimination or addition?

"The Friendly Road," David Grayson; "The Blazed Trail," Stewart Edward White; "Soldiers Three," Kipling; "The Real Dope," Lardner; "Farm Rhymes," Riley; "The Builders and Other Poems," van Dyke; "Life of Washington," Weems; "The Man Without a Country," Hale; "General Zoology," Pearse; "Every Boy's Book of Handicrafts, Sports and Amusements"; "Bird Life," Chapman; "A Guide to the Trees," Lounsberry; Roget's "Thesaurus of English Words and Phrases"; "Putnam's Automobile Handbook"; "A Guide to Mt. Washington"; "Camp Cookery," Kephart; "Rifles and Rifle Shooting," Askins; "Fishing Kits and Equipment," Camp; "French Grammar," Fraser and Squair; "Boy Scouts' Handbook"; "Camping for Boys," Gibson; "Boat Sailers' Manual," Qualtrough; "Botany," Wright; five tree, flower, and bird manuals; twenty books on field and forest; "An American Physician in Turkey," Knapp; "Abraham Lincoln, the Boy and Man," Morgan; "Theodore Roosevelt," William Roscoe Thayer; "World-Wide Bible Study," Cooper; "Sanctified Ones," Stockmayer; "The Victorious Life," Conference addresses; "Young Men Who Overcame," Speer: "Soul Winning Around the World," Alexander; "What is the Gospel?" Trumbull; "David Livingstone," Horne; "Jesus is Coming," Blackstone; "The Bible and its Christ," Torrey; "When Faith Sees Christ," Scofield; "Rightly Dividing the Word of Truth," Scofield; "Victorious Life Studies," McQuilkin; "Their Call to Service," Howard; "The Medical Mission," Wanless; "Secret Prayer," Henry Wright; "The Christian According to Paul," Faris; "Temptation," Howard; "The Way," Pepper;

"Daily Strength for Daily Needs"; "Christianity Is Christ," Griffith Thomas; "James Chalmers," Hall.

These books for the most part were sifted out by the boy himself when he was about sixteen or seventeen, from a collection that represented, better than this remainder can do, the earlier reading of his childhood. Nearly all this reading represents his middle and later teens. You can easily deduce from this group of books many of his interests, and you could discover the tendencies of his life as fairly reflected in the books retained in his own room. Some of those that he read earlier are scattered through the household or are in the possession of younger members of his family.

Here is a bookshelf from the room of a boy in another household, a studious boy, but interested in general rather than specific forms of athletics. These books belong to the period between eleven and seventeen:

The Bible; "Black Beauty," Sewall; "Fairy Tales," Andersen; "Jack the Fire Dog"; "Story of the Bible," Foster; "Cruise of Convention Pilgrims to Palestine"; "My Boys," Alcott; "Hans Brinker," Dodge; "American Life and Adventure"; "Natural History," Woods; "Treasure Island," Stevenson; "The Last of the Mohicans," Cooper; "Hiawatha", "Forging Ahead," "Shifting for Himself," "Strong and Steady," Alger; "Tales from Shakespeare," Lamb; "Piokee and Her People," Jenness; "Birds Worth Knowing," Blanchan; "Airship Boys Adrift"; "Airship Boys' Quest of Aztec Treasure"; "From Ranch to White House," biography of Roosevelt; "The Cruise of the Cachalot," Bullen; "Down the Orinoco in a Canoe"; "The Real Kruger."

Does either collection lack historical works to any unfortunate degree? Would you say that nature studies are over-emphasized, or that possibly there are so many good available books on that subject that the collections increased on that side more than on others? What would you say to the Alger books and others like them? The books that these boys read as required reading in school are not represented here, because many of those in the experience of the first boy were drawn from a neighboring college library, or otherwise borrowed, or drawn from the general library in his home. It is of interest, however, to note that there is hardly a subject represented by any of the books that has not been shared by the fathers with these boys in their reading and activities, not always to the same extent as is represented by the boys' actual attainments, but nevertheless in a very real sense.

It may be interesting to an observer to find that a smaller bookshelf in the first boy's room includes a dozen books that represent the interests that have deepened with him as he has grown older. On this small shelf one finds alongside of a "Library of Wit and Humor," a voluminous report of a Student Volunteer Convention, Kipling's "Collected Poems," and the volume, "The New Morning," which contains numerous poems by Alfred Noyes. There are books on more mature phases of the religious life and in the field of pure literature, and the boy's study Bibles, so that it is apparent that the interests which were developed in the boy's earlier teens, and perhaps even earlier than that, have had naturally a consistent development in what are now his college days.

Turning the pages back a little in the record of this first boy's reading life, this incident may be significant. When he was seven years old his father took him on a little tour of the Book Department of John Wanamaker's store in Phila-delphia. While examining the books there, Mr. Wanamaker, who was well known to the boy's father, greeted the two, and soon it developed that it was the youngster's birthday.

"Oh, I must give him a book," said Mr. Wanamaker. "What would he like?" And he turned expectantly to the boy.

The little fellow looked up in the great merchant's kindly face and said cheerily, "A fairy story."

"A fairy story?" exclaimed Mr. Wanamaker. "Why, you don't want that, do you? You will read it just once and then you will never pick it up again."

The boy shook his head and said nothing.

"Now, what kind of a book would you really like?" asked the merchant.

Looking up again in the same way the little fellow replied quietly, "A fairy story."

Mr. Wanamaker smiled. "Well," he said, "I shall have to get him one." So he took the boy by the hand and wan-dered about among the book tables, finally leading him into a little room set apart for the finest editions. After a time he reappeared and brought the boy back to the waiting father, who watched the whole scene with much interest and curios-ity. "There," said Mr. Wanamaker, "I have given him a fairy story, as you see. And since it is the boy's birthday I think I must send to his mother a book just for herself." And he gave to the boy for his mother a beautiful copy of Stevenson's "A Child's Garden of Verses." There was no escape from the fairy story, and both men knew well enough that there ought not to be any attempted escape too seriously undertaken. There in the heart of the great store stood the distinguished man of acknowledged leadership, attained not only because of his marvelous energy but because of his constructive imagination, as every one knows who knows him at all; and beside him the little boy, eager-eyed and alert, holding in his small hand the new "Green Book of Fairy Tales," an imaginative little fellow, with life an unwritten book for him, while poems quite suited to his age were thoughtfully given to the mother who would be sure to read them aloud to the little boy.

You do have a care in guiding your boy in the choice of his playmates and chums. But are you as keen about helping the youngster from the very beginning in his choice of books?

It may be of interest to many fathers whose attention has not been called to good book lists, to be reminded that Mr. Franklin K. Mathiews has done exceptionally fine work in connection with the Boy Scout movement in preparing reading lists for boys. Then, too, one can find extremely interesting material in this connection in a book called "Children's Books and Reading," by Montrose J. Moses, in which there is a somewhat extended history of the development of books for children, together with a number of suggested book lists. Among these book lists there are numerous ones indicated as published by various libraries or groups or individuals that have made a special study of books for the young. Many individual books are suggested also in the appendix. Another book that will be found of interest to any student of boy life who wants to have on hand a bibliography by means of which he may carry forward his studies of the boy, including a boy's reading, is "A Classified Biography of Boy Life and Organized Work with Boys," by Ronald Tuttle Veal, recently published by Association Press, 347 Madison Avenue, New York. This is said to be "the most complete list of boys' work material in the field, every part of which is made immediately available by the use of a scientific method of classification."

In all our study of the boy's reading, it may be well to revert to the six chief points given in this brief study, and let them have the fullest possible consideration in our thinking; for fatherhood is decidedly incomplete unless it reaches far into a boy's book companionship intellectually, sympathetically, and whole-heartedly.

V

TAKING HIM INTO YOUR CONFIDENCE

THERE is too much mystery about father. You know how it was with yourself. Many a time you wondered what father's business was really like; who and why were the men who called sometimes to see him; and why and where father went when he took the night train, and a few days later came home from a journey with talk about a city, and "conferences" (whatever those are) and seeming particularly glad to get home. "Who is that man?" asked a youngster —very young, of course "who comes here to stay sometimes?" In amazement the mother replied, "Why, that's your father!" But the child had asked what seemed to the child mind a needed question, for that father had been away in pursuance of his calling so steadily or bad reached home after the children's bedtime, and so often left early, that the littlest hardly knew him.

Are you a mystery to your small boy? Does he wonder what you do? If one of his friends should ask him about you, could he give even an approximately intelligent answer? And if he does know the name of your business or profession, does be know anything of its demands upon you, or of what you are trying to do in it?

One of the ablest men I ever knew had a son who in the boy's early twenties was inducted into the father's business. That son, who became his father's successor, once told me that as a small boy he never had the slightest idea as to what his father really did at the office, and he knew very little more about the mystery when he was in his college days. It was only after he had entered into his father's business that he began to understand what had kept that father so busy. He never, indeed, could have understood fully until he had seen it all from the inside; but he declared that his boyhood remoteness from any real touch with the work made it doubly hard for him to grasp the significance of it after he had entered upon his duties. Nor did he know his father as well as both could have wished. The mystery, not intentionally created, was not a relief to the boy in keeping him free from premature care, but a hindrance that delayed for several years his grasp of the work itself and a needed comprehension of his father's activities.

We fathers hardly realize what sharp contrasts there are among us in this aspect of the precious relation of father and son. One New England farmer almost always maintained that his boys could not do the farm work as it ought to be done. They might try, of course; but he himself slaved early and late to do the things he might have taught them to do. It was a mental slant of his to keep boys just outside the enthusiastic expectant training of their highest possibilities, by letting them understand that there were some things quite beyond them. One son pushed his energetic way upward in spite of this training, while the other son deteriorated under it until the day came when the first son was supporting his father's family, and for the most part the brother and his family.

On the other hand, Dr. W. W. Faris, in "The Christian Home," tells this incident of another farmer:

"A father was driving with his growing boy across country new to him. 'Son, how do you like the lay of this land? Does it lie right for good crops? If so, what crops? In what direction does it slope?' The lad, unused to observing in such matters, finally made out enough to say, 'It slopes southeast.' 'Well, how is that for corn?' The son at once saw the point, noted how gentle the slope was, and ventured to reply with some boldness, 'I should think it would be good for corn.' 'Yes, but what about the soil? Is it good soil for corn, or is it too light and sandy?' The boy looked again, and closely: 'Not so sandy as some we passed away back.' 'Not so bad,' said the father; 'but you haven't been used to noting such things. Better cultivate the habit.'"

What was the difference, fundamentally, in the attitude of these farmers toward their sons? Was it in their contrasting ideas as to oneness with their boys, in their readiness to bring their sons as far as possible up to the same level of intelligent deductions from experience that they as fathers had reached? Was it in the first case a question of a certain degree of remoteness from the sons, and in the second, an intimate fellowship with the accompanying desire and purpose to pass on to the boy the father's best in the direction of their interest together?

Of course, it could easily be an unwise practise to unfold prematurely to a growing boy the details of a father's duties and concerns and burdens. There is good reason for guarding a boy from a too early, and therefore necessarily unbalanced disclosure of the sharp disappointments, the severe grind, the sometimes painful disillusionments of the "little journey in the world" upon which father and son have set out; and it is equally needful to guard the boy from the necessarily futile attempts to comprehend at their full value the shining moments of manhood's mountain experiences, save as they may be seen with the zest of vision that belongs always to the youthful explorer. There are some things one cannot know apart from mature experience. But all this cannot fairly be taken as a reason for shutting out the boy from anything that the father ought to pass on to him. There are, as an American essayist has pointed out, "honorable points of ignorance" for us all. Yet the thoughtful father will realize that just as rapidly as the boy's development will permit, he should enter increasingly into his father's fullest confidence.

In no realm of human mystery is the growing boy more curious and sensitive than in all that pertains to sex. In nothing, I think it may be safely said, is the average father more reluctant, more remiss, more helpless and blind, than in dealing with his son's rightful desire to know the foundation sex facts, yet there is no subject touching our human relationships and God's plan for our lives, save the one supreme question of a boy's primary relation to Christ, that brings father and son into such an intimacy as that in which the father takes his son into his confidence on the sex problems that every boy must face.

Many of us have been afraid to do it. That is the plain truth. We are afraid of telling too early the essentials of sex, and we are afraid that we may not know how to tell the story properly and wisely at any time. But there are two things of which we *have* reason enough to be afraid: our own blind notion that somehow it will all come out right, and our own fear of tackling the task. *Not to try to help the growing boy in this is infinitely worse than not doing it as well as we might wish.* We can harm him more by silence than we are at all likely to harm him by premature knowledge. As a matter of tested fact, no father need to bother his head very much about the danger of thrusting this subject upon his young son as one about which the boy is not thinking. The probability is that by the time the father makes up his mind to give his son the needful sex facts, the son will have heard enough that is misleading and vile to give the father a man's job in up-rooting the choking weeds. Why, man, wasn't it so with you, when you were a youngster? What would you give today to get memory entirely clear of the tarnish that came before you were ten years old? Your white-souled little boy, with his glad face, and fine spirit, and loving ways, is no more exempt than you were, and perhaps just now not so separate as you may have been from the atmosphere of contamination. There seems to be a moral soft-coal smoke in the very air of our social conditions that turns to a dull gray any new snow-fall, It makes a great difference whether your boy knows the wonderful story of sex truth from you or a drab perversion of the story from the ignorant or worse.

Yes, there are books a boy can read—good ones, too, on this theme. But why a book for your boy at first, when he has his father and wants his father more than some of us realize? A boy in his teens ran across some good sex books in the home library. He glanced through one or two of them somewhat curiously and then put them back on the shelf. His mother noticed the boy's mild interest, and asked him what he thought of the books. "Oh, they're pretty good," he replied casually, "but I don't need them; father has told me all that long ago." Incidentally, the books had helped "father" very much in talking with the boy, but the books were not allowed to do the talking first. Was that father wise or not? Would you prefer to tell your boy the facts or hand him a book?

There are glad surprises in store for the father who will face the issue squarely and take the boy into his confidence. I cannot dare to name the exact age at which the wonder of birth should be in part explained. I do not venture to suggest precisely how much shall be told. Generalizations as to the boy whom you know, or ought to know, best are not altogether safe for an outsider. But curiosity as to the way in which babies come is common among children, and silly and lying explanations are always bad. The very small boy is quite content at first with the frankly stated and perfectly honest assertion that God has sent the new baby. Not that curiosity is wholly allayed, but the fact is acceptable and accepted. And parents do not have to shake the confidence of their children a few years later by denying that fact, as they must do when a lie is told at first, and the truth comes out later.

In a large meeting of pastors and Sunday-school superintendents the leader called upon a personal friend of his to tell the story of that friend's experience in unfolding for his small boys the beautiful mystery of birth. And this, in substance, was the story:

"We were in Italy at the time. I do not know just what led the older boy to ask questions on the subject just then, but it was during a vacation period when we were together as a family, and it was down by the lakeside on Como that the youngster asked me if I could tell him how babies are born. I saw that the moment had come when his interest in the question was keen and reasonable, so I asked him to go with me to our rooms, and there overlooking the lake we sat by the wide windows while I told him much of the wonderful birth story.

"I was led to make the whole occasion as natural and beautiful as I could, and so I reminded him of the flowers and birds that he loved, the nests with the delicate eggs resting in them; the young birds coming from the eggs; the chickens under the care of the mother hen; the kittens that he had often seen as the mother cat fed them and watched over them.

"The boy listened as sedately as one could wish. He glanced over the lake to the mountains beyond; he gazed steadily into my eyes and nodded with an occasional 'Yes, I see,' until I said that very much as the mothers of whom I had been telling him brought their little ones into the world, so the baby's mother cared for the little baby life within her own dear body, keeping him safe close to her own heart—then the boy's eyes opened wide. I told of the months of care before the baby could live out in the light and air like the rest, and that finally when he had grown to be just such a small baby as the boy had often seen, he was ready to leave the mother's body by a way God had prepared. 'So you see,' I said very quietly, 'why it is that I have always told you how much I loved my own mother, and why any boy,'—but the boy was standing now, his eyes flashing with excitement. His hands were clenched and he began to stride up and down the room. What had happened to him? Was it all a blunder to tell him so much?

"'Oh, oh! Isn't that wonderful, isn't that wonderful!' he was saying. 'I don't wonder you loved your mother!' Then his voice choked; and what he said about his own mother is one of the confidences of father and son. I can never forget the scene, as the child, all elate with the revelation of the mystery of sonship and mother-love, fairly glowed with the fervor of a new and understanding purpose to know his mother as never before. And that was an hour of mountain outlook, new intimacy, and opening channels for later frank talks between us. An almost identical experience was a similar conversation with the younger brother, and with complete breaking down of any wrong reserve between father and sons on the problem that involves such far-reaching issues for the growing boy."

When the story was finished, one after another in that company of mature men spoke with intense feeling of the need they remembered in their own lives, and of the need of exalting today to its rightful place in a boy's home training a sound sex knowledge. Of course the day will come in any boy's development when he will need to understand the details very fully lest he should fall into habits that have worse teeth than any steel trap ever had. And the father ought to rejoice in the privilege of telling his boy whatever he ought to know on the subject.

And what would it be worth in the long run to us fathers and our boys to have each one of the boys honestly able and glad to say, "I can tell my father anything. I can go to my father about anything, and never be sorry that I have put up to him what I want to know"?

VI

WHAT GUESTS SHALL HE MEET?

WITH no less care than we admit books to our homes, must we invite guests to share in the fellowship of our family life. Of course we cannot always choose our guests, for "the house by the side of the road" would not fulfill its mission if it were to entertain only those congenial folks whose presence is always a delight. The home has a mission beyond its chosen favorites, and in this the children may well learn to share.

Childhood's own guests are often examples of the action of a democratic spirit that ought not to be too quickly or carelessly discouraged. Boys and girls alike will choose their own guests with a delightful disregard of the conventions, and some playmates and "callers" that are adroitly chosen for them may get anything but a cordial reception. A small girl was seen by her mother to be progressing rapidly in an intimacy with a child from a neighboring city household. The new little girl seemed well-mannered and modest, and not undesirable. "Who is that little girl you are playing with so much?" asked the young mother. "Oh, that is the cook's child at the Smiths' house" was the matter-of-fact answer. It appeared also that she was a very good child, and much liked by the little girl. And why not? The little girl is now grown into young womanhood and is loved for her friendly, democratic ways, and honored for her unassuming, straightforward Christian graces. She has real friends among the lowly and the—

well, otherwise. Her guests are of many types; but one notices that they are girls who love the best things in their forward look. Was the democracy of her childhood, guarded as it was in questions of character, a detriment or a help?

Consider the case of two boys from the same neighborhood, one living in a city home of quiet comfort and unfailing hospitality, the other dwelling in a great house with lavish evidences of wealth all around him. The little rich boy was a guest in the home of the other boy one day, and as he moved about the house, his glance took in the simplicity of it, and with a touch of pity in his voice he said to his host, "Contrast this house with ours!" The boy of the modest home said nothing, because he did not know what to say. But his sense of hospitality was a bit strained. A "cook's child" would not have been likely to forget so his place as a guest. Is it probable that the small boy from the lavish house had never been trained in the courtesies of hospitality in his own home? And might not more home training as host have made him more acceptable as a guest?

There are tragedies bleak and painful in the memory of some grown-up children in the parental introduction of certain unforgotten guests. Childhood is jealous of its own interests, and claims the right of self-protection from guests who don't "belong." I well remember the rage and chagrin that seized me when, at the manly age of eight, I was summoned by my mother to receive as my "callers"—not hers at all—two very admirable and kindly little girls about three years my senior who wanted simply to be neighborly with the newcomers in a country town. Girls calling to see me! No, sir I wouldn't see them. And finally, gently mothered into it, I